The God of My Life

A devotional colouring book

Michael Parsons
with illustrations by
Mike Coltman

BRF

The Bible Reading Fellowship
15 The Chambers, Vineyard
Abingdon OX14 3FE
brf.org.uk

The Bible Reading Fellowship (BRF) is a Registered Charity (233280)

ISBN 978 0 85746 584 9
First published 2017
10 9 8 7 6 5 4 3 2 1 0
All rights reserved

Acknowledgements
Unless otherwise stated, all scripture quotations taken from The Holy Bible, New
International Version (Anglicised edition) copyright © 1979, 1984, 2011 by Biblica. Used by
permission of Hodder & Stoughton Publishers, a Hachette UK company. All rights reserved.
'NIV' is a registered trademark of Biblica. UK trademark number 1448790.

Scripture quotations taken from *THE MESSAGE*, copyright © 1993, 1994, 1995, 1996, 2000,
2001, 2002 by Eugene H. Peterson. Used by permission of NavPress. All rights reserved.
Represented by Tyndale House Publishers, Inc.

Every effort has been made to trace and contact copyright owners for material used in
this resource. We apologise for any inadvertent omissions or errors, and would ask those
concerned to contact us so that full acknowledgement can be made in the future.

A catalogue record for this book is available from the British Library

Printed and bound by CPI Group (UK) Ltd, Croydon CR0 4YY

Introduction

When the phone rings at my work desk, my immediate response is to pick up a pen and a rough piece of paper. I do this to write notes so I don't forget what's being said, but also to doodle because I find that doodling concentrates the mind, helps me to focus better and encourages thought. A lot of people find the same with colouring in: it focuses the mind, allowing you to think without distraction.

That's the simple basis for this devotional resource. The hope is that colouring in will be a small exercise in mindfulness, in being absorbed into the moment, into the present, so that your thinking will focus and run with the thoughts offered in both the psalm and the reflections that follow the psalm.

So, why not start by reading the whole psalm indicated at the top of the page? Follow this by concentrating on the specific verses and the reflection given. While you're colouring in the pictures, you could ponder what you've read, trying not to be distracted by anything outside of the immediate experience. In this way, by the Lord's grace, you might well find that the psalmist's thoughts about God and his relationship to him become your own. And don't forget to pray as you start, asking God to enrich your thinking and, through that, your relationship with him.

> **Open my eyes that I may see**
> **wonderful things in your law.**
> PSALM 119:18

A note on the use of pens

While the paper for this colouring book has been selected with care, there is the possibility of ink show-through if pressure is applied too heavily when using felt-tip pens. We therefore recommend the use of coloured pencils, as they will not smudge or bleed. If you are using a felt-tip pen, we recommend you test it somewhere unobtrusive (for example, at the back of the book) and keep your strokes light and sweeping. It is advisable to avoid permanent markers or any pen with a heavy ink flow.

Confidence in God

Psalm 3

But you, Lord, are a shield around me,
my glory, the One who lifts my head high.
I call out to the Lord,
and he answers me from his holy mountain.

PSALM 3:3–4

In a situation of danger and threat, the psalmist finds his confidence in God alone. Even in such a predicament, he is able to rest in the Lord who answers prayer (v. 4).

What troubling situations do you face, or have you faced in the past? Though your circumstances are unlikely to be the same as David's, God is still the same. Are you able to find confidence in the Lord, your protector (v. 3)? Why not rest in him today?

The mindfulness of God

Psalm 8

> When I consider your heavens,
>   the work of your fingers,
> the moon and the stars,
>   which you have set in place,
> what is mankind that you are mindful of them,
>   human beings, that you care for them?

PSALM 8:3–4

Human beings are wonderful, aren't we? Made just a little lower than angels, created in dust, crowned with glory, set in the immeasurable context of the universe, God-cherished.

Is that how you feel today? Are you aware of the 'glory' (the worth) in which God considers you? How might this affect your self-image today? The Lord cares for you with overwhelming and fatherly love.

Love for God

Psalm 18

I love you, Lord, my strength.
The Lord is my rock, my fortress and my deliverer;
   my God is my rock, in whom I take refuge,
   my shield and the horn of my salvation, my stronghold…
For who is God besides the Lord?
   And who is the Rock except our God?

PSALM 18:1–2, 31

What a declaration of love for God! The psalm shows that David loves God because God is involved in every aspect of his life: more, the Lord delights in David (v. 19).

Do you love God? There is no one like him (v. 31). Are you aware of his presence in your life and his delight in you? Why not ask for a sense of his love towards you?

The God who speaks to us

Psalm 19

The heavens declare the glory of God;
  the skies proclaim the work of his hands...
The law of the Lord is perfect,
  refreshing the soul.
PSALM 19:1, 7

The psalmist rejoices because God speaks to us. He's not a speechless idol; he reaches out to humanity, accommodates our humanness and reveals himself through created things and words.

Has the Lord spoken to you today or in the past? In what ways might you listen more attentively to his wonderful voice?

Seeking God's face

Psalm 24

They will receive blessing from the Lord
and vindication from God their Saviour.
Such is the generation of those who seek him,
who seek your face, God of Jacob.
PSALM 24:5–6

The psalmist wants us to know that to stand before such a God (see vv. 1, 8–10) is to seek his face, to have faith, to receive grace, to live lives worthy of our calling (v. 4).

Are you seeking God in this way? How do you think this might be increasingly seen in day-to-day living and relationships?

Worship God

Psalm 29

Ascribe to the Lord, you heavenly beings,
   ascribe to the Lord glory and strength.
Ascribe to the Lord the glory due to his name;
   worship the Lord in the splendour of his holiness.

PSALM 29:1–2

The Lord is worthy of our worship not merely because he is glorious, majestic, creative, all-powerful and so on, but also because he gives his people longed-for peace (v. 11).

Do you long for peace in your life? What would it mean for you today? Why not pray to the Lord for that blessing?

The forgiveness of God

Psalm 32

Blessed is the one
    whose transgressions are forgiven,
    whose sins are covered.
Blessed is the one
    whose sin the Lord does not count against them
    and in whose spirit is no deceit.

PSALM 32:1–2

It couldn't be clearer: when the psalmist honestly confessed his sins to the Lord (v. 5) he was forgiven. Knowing the Lord's unfailing love brings joy, a sense of divine presence.

Do you know the joy of the Lord's gracious forgiveness and the release (vv. 3–5) that it brings? The psalmist prayed for it. Today may be your opportunity to do so too.

Hope in God

Psalm 33

We wait in hope for the Lord;
he is our help and our shield.
In him our hearts rejoice,
for we trust in his holy name.
May your unfailing love be with us, Lord,
even as we put our hope in you.
PSALM 33:20–22

The psalmist states that we can hope and wait on God because God is trustworthy; after all, he created everything (v. 9), he is involved in the world, his is covenant love (v. 12).

Is there something you wait and hope for? Are you trusting the Lord in this? Be convinced of his faithful love in this context; after all, he is our God, our Father.

Thirsting for God

Psalm 42

As the deer pants for streams of water,
so my soul pants for you, my God.
My soul thirsts for God, for the living God.
When can I go and meet with God?

PSALM 42:1–2

Downcast, the psalmist remembers past times of experiencing closeness with the Lord. He tells his soul, his inmost being, to hope in God.

Do you long for God like a deer longing for clean water in a dry, barren and parched landscape? The psalmist does because God is 'the God of my life' (v. 8). What is it about the Lord and your relationship with him that would encourage you to long after him in this way?

God our refuge

Psalm 46

God is our refuge and strength,
  an ever-present help in trouble.
Therefore we will not fear, though the earth give way
  and the mountains fall into the heart of the sea,
though its waters roar and foam
  and the mountains quake with their surging.
PSALM 46:1–3

It is because the psalmist has experienced God's protection and help in difficult times that he affirms he will not fear. The exaggerated imagery underlines his confidence.

It is all too easy to be fearful in the world, or in our own circumstances. The Lord would have us be still and know that he is God (v. 10). Today, trust in him, your 'refuge and strength'.

Starting again with God

Psalm 51

Create in me a pure heart, O God,
   and renew a steadfast spirit within me.
Do not cast me from your presence
   or take your Holy Spirit from me.
Restore to me the joy of your salvation
   and grant me a willing spirit, to sustain me.

PSALM 51:10–12

The psalm's thought pivots around the word 'create'. *THE MESSAGE* Bible translation has, 'God, make a fresh start in me, shape a Genesis week from the chaos of my life.'

Sometimes we feel that the only way to go forward is to go back and start again. Is that the way you sometimes feel? Do you feel that today? Ask Creator God to work in your life by his gracious and powerful Spirit.

Trust in God

Psalm 56

When I am afraid, I put my trust in you.
  In God, whose word I praise –
in God I trust and am not afraid.
  What can mere mortals do to me?
PSALM 56:3–4

The psalmist has enemies who wish him harm, but he knows that God is *for* him, not against him (v. 9). Therefore, he trusts; he will not be afraid.

Though your situation is probably very different, where do you put your trust? Do you know, even today, that God is *for* you, not against you? That makes all the difference.

Longing for God

Psalm 63

You, God, are my God,
   earnestly I seek you;
I thirst for you,
   my whole being longs for you,
in a dry and parched land
   where there is no water.

PSALM 63:1

Having experienced the power and glory of God (v. 2), the psalmist's whole being is taken up in longing and praise: his soul, his body, his hands and lips (vv. 4–5).

Have you experienced God in your life? When? What was it like? Does it fill you with worship? Why not reflect on the Lord's goodness and spend time praising him today?

Praise for God

Psalm 66

Shout for joy to God, all the earth!
  Sing the glory of his name;
  make his praise glorious.
Say to God, 'How awesome are your deeds!'...
Praise be to God,
  who has not rejected my prayer
  or withheld his love from me!

PSALM 66:1–3, 20

When we come to faith, we find our story in that of the Bible. As the psalmist rehearses Israel's narrative (vv. 6–12), we see something of God's goodness to us.

Israel's testimony of divine grace results in joy and praise. What does your testimony look like? Does it still resound to the praise of a gracious God?

The blessing of God

Psalm 67

**May God be gracious to us and bless us
and make his face to shine on us –
so that your ways may be known on earth,
your salvation among all nations.
May the peoples praise you, God;
may all the peoples praise you.**

PSALM 67:1–3

The psalmist yearns for the Lord to bless him and his people, in order that the world may come to see the goodness of God and praise him.

We often seek divine blessing, but how often do we long for it so that the world may come to acknowledge the Lord and worship him? Might this thought affect your relationships with those who do not yet have faith?

To be near God

Psalm 73

Whom have I in heaven but you?
  And earth has nothing I desire besides you.
My flesh and my heart may fail,
  but God is the strength of my heart
  and my portion for ever...
But as for me, it is good to be near God.

PSALM 73:25–26, 28

Like many of us, when things are not going well, the psalmist compares his life to that of others. At one level he finds it wanting, until he considers how good it is to be near God.

We all make this comparison at times. Others seem to have it all. We wonder whether it's worth having faith. Why not take the time to pause and reflect on your relationship with the Lord?

Questioning the love of God

Psalm 77

I cried out to God for help;
  I cried out to God to hear me.
When I was in distress, I sought the Lord;
  at night I stretched out untiring hands,
  and I would not be comforted…
'Will the Lord reject for ever?
  Will he never show his favour again?'

PSALM 77:1–2, 7

The psalmist goes through a difficult period of apparent rejection by God. The Lord feels absent, somehow against him and forgetful of the Lord's own mercy.

We can sometimes feel that way too. Notice the psalmist's persistence and deliberate recalling of past grace. How is your experience of God today? What past grace might you remember to be assured of future goodness?

God's dwelling place

Psalm 84

How lovely is your dwelling-place,
  Lord Almighty!
My soul yearns, even faints,
  for the courts of the Lord;
my heart and my flesh cry out
  for the living God.

PSALM 84:1–2

The psalmist longs to be in the presence of God, to sense his nearness and to be at an intimate distance. For him, the temple in Jerusalem is the physical location of that.

Is there a particular physical place that helps you sense the presence of God? A church or cathedral, perhaps? A room in your house? Beside the sea, or among a mountain range? Why is this so?

God's gracious restoration

Psalm 85

> Restore us again, God our Saviour,
>   and put away your displeasure towards us.
> Will you be angry with us for ever?…
> Will you not revive us again,
>   that your people may rejoice in you?
> Show us your unfailing love, Lord,
>   and grant us your salvation.

PSALM 85:4–7

Resting on Israel's previous experience of divine renewal (vv. 1–3), the psalmist pleads with the God of their salvation that he might restore them again to faith.

Sadly, we sometimes fall from the Lord's grace, too. The psalmist reminds us that when we ask for blessing, we should not return to folly (v. 8).

Praying to God

Psalm 86

Hear me, Lord, and answer me,
  for I am poor and needy.
Guard my life, for I am faithful to you;
  save your servant who trusts in you.
You are my God; have mercy on me, Lord,
  for I call to you all day long.
Bring joy to your servant, Lord,
  for I put my trust in you.

PSALM 86:1–4

David's confidence that God will answer his prayer is based squarely on who the Lord is (see vv. 10, 15, for example), on their relationship and on his own perseverance.

Is your praying confident? Are you able to rest on who God is for you? Do you persist in prayer (see v. 3)? Ask God for a sign of his goodness (v. 17).

The favour of God

Psalm 90

**May the favour of the Lord our God rest on us;
establish the work of our hands for us –
yes, establish the work of our hands.**

PSALM 90:17

The psalmist appears only too aware of the brevity of life, the shortness of our existence: like grass we spring up at daylight, only to wither at evening (vv. 5–6).

It is in that sobering context that he asks for God's favour, that he might give some worth to his short life. How might your life be 'established' by God? Consider: your life's worth and satisfaction is wrapped up in God's love (v. 14).

The Lord reigns

Psalm 93

The Lord reigns, he is robed in majesty;
**   The Lord is robed in majesty and armed with strength;**
**   indeed, the world is established, firm and secure.**
Your throne was established long ago;
**   you are from all eternity.**

PSALM 93:1–2

The psalmist says that the Lord reigns and backs up that declaration with the fact that he is 'robed in majesty', 'armed with strength', seated on a throne. He says too that the world is established, 'firm and secure'.

Acknowledging the fragility of the world today, how does it help us to know that God reigns, that his statutes 'stand firm' (v. 5)? How does that help us to pray to him in times of difficulty and distress?

People of God's pasture

Psalm 95

> Come, let us bow down in worship,
>   let us kneel before the Lord our Maker;
> for he is our God
>   and we are the people of his pasture,
>   the flock under his care.
>
> PSALM 95:6–7

Music, singing, joy, shouting, bowing, kneeling, worship! All because the psalmist knows that God is the maker, both of creation and of the nation of Israel: his people, his flock.

The premise of all this is that 'he is our God' (v. 7); not simply 'God', but '*our* God'; we are 'under his care'. Why not think through what this means to you today? Maybe you'll finish in worship.

The Lord is God

Psalm 100

Enter his gates with thanksgiving
    and his courts with praise;
        give thanks to him and praise his name.
For the Lord is good and his love endures forever;
    his faithfulness continues through all generations.

PSALM 100:4–5

Here the psalmist encourages people to come before God with grateful praise. The reason he gives is simple: God is unchangingly good.

How has the Lord been unchangingly good to you, both in the past and the present? Perhaps you could spend some time reflecting on the ways.

The forbearance of God

Psalm 103

The Lord is compassionate and gracious,
  slow to anger, abounding in love.
He will not always accuse,
  nor will he harbour his anger for ever;
he does not treat us as our sins deserve
  or repay us according to our iniquities.
For as high as the heavens are above the earth,
  so great is his love for those who fear him;
as far as the east is from the west,
  so far has he removed our transgressions from us.

PSALM 103:8–12

The psalmist is persuaded of God's forgiveness; all his sins are forgiven (v. 3). All that he is, his 'inmost being' (v. 1), blesses God because of this precious truth.

Why not ponder these well-known verses in relation to your own life and experience of the Lord's compassion?

The works of God

Psalm 111

Praise the Lord.
I will extol the Lord with all my heart
   in the council of the upright and in the assembly.
Great are the works of the Lord;
   they are pondered by all who delight in them.

PSALM 111:1–2

What 'works' is the psalmist praising God for in this psalm? He mentions the Lord's provision, his covenant (v. 5), his protection (v. 6), his salvation (v. 9), his faithful love seen in their lives (vv. 8–9).

Those who delight in God ponder his deeds, the psalmist says. Why not ponder his deeds in your own life and in the lives of those you love?

The glory of God

Psalm 115

Not to us, Lord, not to us
but to your name be the glory,
because of your love and faithfulness…
May you be blessed by the Lord,
the Maker of heaven and earth.

PSALM 115:1, 15

Unlike the useless idols of other nations, God is in heaven with power and authority. Unlike them, he speaks, he hears, he remembers, he creates and he blesses. The glory goes to him alone.

Does the repetition of 'not to us… not to us' (v. 1) imply anything, perhaps? How can we make sure the glory (worth, acknowledgement) goes to God alone?

The help of God

Psalm 121

I lift up my eyes to the mountains –
   where does my help come from?
My help comes from the Lord,
   the Maker of heaven and earth.

PSALM 121:1–2

The psalmist declares that his help comes from no one other than the Lord, the 'Maker of heaven and earth', the one who watches over everything he does (vv. 7–8).

If the Lord is as the psalmist says, why would we look elsewhere for help? Are you able to prioritise the Lord in this, knowing that he cares immensely for you?

Looking to God

Psalm 123

I lift up my eyes to you,
   to you who sit enthroned in heaven.
As the eyes of slaves look to the hand of their master,
   as the eyes of a female slave look to the hand of her mistress,
so our eyes look to the Lord our God,
   till he shows us his mercy.

PSALM 123:1–2

The psalmist has been ridiculed (v. 4). Repeating the phrase 'Have mercy on us' (v. 3) implies that he's endured this contempt for a long time. He's prayed and waited.

Waiting on the Lord's answer seems so passive sometimes. But the psalmist shows that to wait is to be attentive, actively looking for God's response, for it *will* come.

Waiting for God

Psalm 130

> I wait for the Lord, my whole being waits,
>   and in his word I put my hope.
> I wait for the Lord
>   more than watchmen wait for the morning,
>   more than watchmen wait for the morning.
>
> PSALM 130:5–6

The psalmist's image brings to mind a night-shift worker anticipating the end of the shift – but with more at stake. Watchmen help guard a city against attack. He hopes, and his whole being waits.

The psalmist cries from a miserable place (v. 1). But he hopes, because he knows the Lord's willingness to forgive (vv. 3–4). Be assured that the Lord loves you. In that context, what do you wait for from him? For what do you hope?

God's blessing of unity

Psalm 133

How good and pleasant it is
    when God's people live together in unity!
It is like precious oil poured on the head,
    running down on the beard,
running down on Aaron's beard,
    down on the collar of his robe.
It is as if the dew of Hermon
    were falling on Mount Zion.
For there the Lord bestows his blessing,
    even life for evermore.

PSALM 133:1–3

Two great images! Oil covering the priest and dew covering the mountain. Unity between those who believe in God is all pervasive; it is a blessing of God in and to a fractured world.

Consider in what ways you are part of that divine blessing. Are unity and peace characteristics of your life?

The thoughts of God

Psalm 139

> How precious to me are your thoughts, God!
>> How vast is the sum of them!
> Were I to count them,
>> they would outnumber the grains of the sand –
>> when I awake, I am still with you.

PSALM 139:17–18

In this psalm, the writer may appear to be trying to escape God for some reason (v. 8); but, in fact, he's rejoicing that the Lord is utterly familiar with him and with all his ways.

Imagine a sandy beach, miles long. Pick up a handful of sand – a miniscule fraction of the whole. Attempt the impossible task of counting the grains in your hand. Ponder that God's good thoughts about you are uncountable.

Complaining to God

Psalm 142

> I cry aloud to the Lord;
>   I lift up my voice to the Lord for mercy.
> I pour out before him my complaint;
>   before him I tell my trouble.
>
> PSALM 142:1–2

In danger of his life, the psalmist complains to God. He protests, but retains his faith: God watches over him (v. 3), he is his refuge (v. 5) and he longs to worship him (v. 7).

Although the difficulties in our lives may not be the same as those in the psalmist's, our lives can be bitter, disappointing and taxing on our faith. Do you ever feel like this? Do you feel like it today? Who is God for you when you complain?

A life entrusted to God

Psalm 143

Let the morning bring me word of your unfailing love,
    for I have put my trust in you.
Show me the way I should go,
    for to you I entrust my life…
may your good Spirit
    lead me on level ground.

PSALM 143:8, 10

As the Lord's servant (v. 12) and knowing him to be 'good' (v. 10), the psalmist entrusts his whole life to God; he 'hides' in him (v. 9).

Sometimes we find it difficult to know God's guidance for our lives. We want him to lead us 'on level ground'. Does this describe you today? Trust him. Know that he's good.

The wonderful works of God

Psalm 145

Great is the Lord and most worthy of praise;
  his greatness no one can fathom.
One generation commends your works to another;
  they tell of your mighty acts.
They speak of the glorious splendour of your majesty –
  and I will meditate on your wonderful works.

PSALM 145:3–5

The whole psalm speaks of the works of God – full of goodness and love, forgiveness, care and faithfulness, righteousness and salvation.

No wonder the psalmist promises to meditate on the works of God, to proclaim them to others, to celebrate them (vv. 5–7). Why not tell someone today about the Lord's goodness towards you? Who would you choose? How would you say it?

Lifelong praise of God

Psalm 146

Praise the Lord.
Praise the Lord, my soul.
I will praise the Lord all my life;
   I will sing praise to my God as long as I live.
PSALM 146:1–2

The one constant in our lives is God (v. 3). The psalmist speaks of him as faithful forever (v. 6), as reigning forever (v. 10). It seems appropriate, then, to promise to trust him and to worship him wholeheartedly for as long as we can – 'all my life' and 'as long as I live'.

Reflect on the thought that 'all my life' and 'as long as I live' starts for you again today. Worship of the Lord may begin at this moment. The psalmist names him as '*my* God' – why not allow your relationship with the Lord to fill your heart and life with joy and praise?

The universal praise of God

Psalm 148

Let them praise the name of the Lord,
　　for his name alone is exalted;
　　his splendour is above the earth and the heavens.
And he has raised up for his people a horn,
　　the praise of all his faithful servants,
　　of Israel, the people close to his heart.
Praise the Lord.

PSALM 148:13–14

The psalmist says that God not only created everything, but that he cares for everything. Look at the list he gives here in this psalm. He deserves the praise of everything!

But above all else, God calls people to be 'close to his heart' (v. 14). What does this phrase mean to you today? What does it convey of the Lord's relationship with you?

The joyful worship of God

Psalm 150

Praise the Lord.
Praise God in his sanctuary;
   praise him in his mighty heavens.
Praise him for his acts of power;
   praise him for his surpassing greatness.
Praise him with the sounding of the trumpet,
   praise him with the harp and lyre,
praise him with tambourine and dancing,
   praise him with the strings and pipe,
praise him with the clash of cymbals,
   praise him with resounding cymbals.
Let everything that has breath praise the Lord.
Praise the Lord.

PSALM 150:1–6

This short psalm exhorts us, and everything that has breath, to praise the Lord!
Join this wonderful, universal, awestruck and grateful choir (and band!) today,
worshipping God in all that you do.

BRF

Transforming
lives and communities

Christian growth and understanding of the Bible

Resourcing individuals, groups and leaders in churches for their own spiritual journey and for their ministry

Church outreach in the local community

Offering three programmes that churches are embracing to great effect as they seek to engage with their local communities and transform lives

Teaching Christianity in primary schools

Working with children and teachers to explore Christianity creatively and confidently

Children's and family ministry

Working with churches and families to explore Christianity creatively and bring the Bible alive

Visit **brf.org.uk** for more information on BRF's work
Review this book on Twitter using **#BRFconnect**

brf.org.uk

The Bible Reading Fellowship (BRF) is a Registered Charity (No. 233280)